MW01241806

SHAWNVERSATION

BY: Shawn LaVette

ISBN-13:978-1721555499
ISBN-10:1721555498

LAVETTE PUBLISHING LLC.

This collection of poetry represents my own personal truths. This is Shawnversation: conversation from Shawn with a delivery sprouting from the life I have been blessed to live.

Hopefully, my conversation will move you. It is not my fault if you move wrong and I take no responsibility for that. If you move right may God bless me and have mercy on my soul.

LAVETTE PUBLISHING LLC.

PROLOGUE

Greetings,

I'm Shawn. Welcome to a collection of my conversation. This is a unique yet relatable place you've come to; All from me, all from what I've grown to understand or what I've been through. My original or adopted philosophies, all conversation only Shawn can give... All Shawnversation.

I wrote this collection as it came to me wherever I may have been at any given time. The world was my lab for this collection. As the topics came to mind or out of my mouth due to one of life's trials I'd write a piece in line with the message of my conversation or action. I narrowed down the content, choosing to leave you with 36 pieces.

This collection may serve as a reminder for those who will be reminded. Reminded that you were created for excellence; reminded that we are struggling to win just like you. Keep in mind that we are all human beings, growing and living. My writing is my legacy, this is what I leave the world with. My writing and reciting is my impact. You will be moved.

LAVETTE PUBLISHING LLC.

CONTENTS

LAVETTE PUBLISHING LLC.

Comments about SEED

In this piece Shawnversation draws a correlation between a seed and achievement. How life and things in life don't just happen and are a process of many components which come together to produce a desired result. Come together as in work together like compliment and co-depend on the other for achievement to occur. With all this happening in a process during which most of the initial and most vital parts are happening... yet go unseen.

This is exactly why a seed is likened to a dream. The seed doesn't look like it can do all of who and what it transforms into.

Growth.

A seed.

LAVETTE PUBLISHING LLC.

SEED

A seed...
Simple as it may seem...
A seed is a dream:
In wake of all that it must do to achieve.
Take me, and place me, if I be the seed;
Find a good space for me,
Give me... a fair chance...
To be.
Cover me with earth, sprinkle me with water,
In the ground hard enough, with the sun as my starter;
The elements as my engine, with the nourishment that I'm getting,
I grow and I grow for days before you know there is a life coming into
    existence;
From within... Me...
To achieve, to be: Alive.
Me, the seed, I must strive;
Grow towards what I have not;
I stretch my roots down,
So my life can come up and out!
I dig deep, beneath me, from within me,
I go... further...underneath,
So my life can be seen;
As in manifest,
Above the surface,
I've been growing,
Yet, you didn't know it yet;
But you know now!
You know now that I Am;
Here;
Alive, from a seed;
From a simple state of being, so I seemed;
I was placed, and taken, and I strived when you couldn't see.
I grew when you were sleep.
I dug from within myself! Deep.
To be... I tried,

LAVETTE PUBLISHING LLC.

I strived: I am a dream... achieved.
From The Almighty;
The Most High:
The Creator of me.
For no matter how haughty a man may be,
Regardless of his ability to build things,
Man can never, ever create from scratch,
The seemingly simple Seed.

NEGATIVITY...

This is a shout out to negativity. I wrote this reminding myself of what negativity is and where it is: Beneath Me. Beneath you too. We have work to do. We're managers. Managing . We're put here to manage. The first three letters of manager is m-a-n so the idea of the managing concept involves mankind. Let us do what we were put here to do. Don't forget to respond on levels higher than negativity because Negativity is beneath you.

LAVETTE PUBLISHING LLC.

NEGATIVITY

Negativity, Negativity,
Wherefore `art thou Negativity?
Wait...I know...You're in the negative:
Beneath Me.
Can I ask you something?
Why must you attempt to hinder me?
You may delay me – You never stop me;
You wind up under - You never top me;
You just ... You're just:
Negative.
You're an antonym of positive:
An opposite, not similar.
You're synonymous with losers,
Your value isn't equivalent with winners.
Negativity, Negativity,
Whensoever and Wheresoever we meet:
I'll dissect you or deflect you,
But I will never let you live in me;
I will beat you, I will defeat you,
You will always be underneath.
Negativity, Negativity:
You aint got nothing on Me!

LAVETTE PUBLISHING LLC.

I wrote the piece SPECULATION thinking of what it means to apply for a company. Thinking of how I have been the passionate individual in the past who applied for a job. I stressed that I would be the success story, the inexperienced person who will prove themselves. When to be blunt about it: my credentials didn't add up to enough.

Companies have what I call "Disqualifiquestions" . Disqualifying Questions. Each question can either qualify you or disqualify you in an air of speculation. Their policies are set up. I emphasize Policies. Cause it's a policy. A rule. It isn't the HR. The policy is the reason why. Policy is derived from speculation. It isn't even personal but it stings real bad when a disqualifiquestion knocks you upside the head.

I might make this sound easy but understand that I know it isn't easy. Yet I want to encourage you to get yourself on the right side of those disqualifiquestions. Make it where policy is in your favor. You're going to have to work if you intend to reproduce and contribute to your existence so get you Your Qualification. Your stamp. Your what you can do. Be certain that you're going to be able to provide for you and yours and let all Speculate that you CAN. You were created to be able to.

SPECULATION

Concluding on an imaginary basis,
Taking...
The facts, solving the equation,
Without all the numbers,
Only using signs and variables:
Possibilities,
Beliefs and then acting,
From: Speculation.

Since they believe you can, they bet on you. They interview, hire and have you fill out W-2's. All because of the vibe they get and the credentials you possess, since the certificate says this and the degree says that and the resume' reads that you will be the addition the company needs... The company lets you in, lending you the shareholders money betting on you like a gamble. The HR feels you meet the criteria, and are worthy of the risk so he merges you with the company.

But your friend was too risky. He says that he will work but what does he know? How can he tell us he is willing to learn *now* when he had 30 years of opportunity before he turned in the application to obtain the GED, or high school diploma – For free. Before he made it to me – The hypothetical, critical HR – Who's only job is to critique and be sure the "match" is a match in fact and is truly what the company needs in this prospective employee who says he can do *anything* yet his papers don't say anything. Who is he without a trail, without a skill, where has he been and why should I recommend we pay him: The Shareholder's money? Can I put him in the company?

Concluding on an imaginary basis,
Taking... The facts...
Solving the equation,
Without all the numbers,
Only using signs and variables,
Beliefs and then acting,
From: Speculation

LAVETTE PUBLISHING LLC.

I wrote LIFE QUIZ at a time when I was going through a set of trials which I had never experienced. It was tough. Was having insurance woes. Pay insurance payments from every check but then I need to have surgery on a fractured Scaphoid bone now I had to pay a deductible before I have the surgery. $2500

Then the doctor comes to talk to me about the surgery saying that after he seen the Xrays he agrees with the Physicians Assistant and that we would proceed with the surgery. "if you have any questions about the procedure Mister Lavette" he said as he wrote down the name of the procedure on a card "You can look it up and that should answer all your questions".

"Look it up like what" I asked "Like google it?"

In so many words he said yes.

I fired him and went to an entirely different doctor. Tell me to google the procedure when I'm paying him to cut on me. Not with my money.

Then in the midst of my working to earn the money there were countless hang ups and issues delaying the process and for each one I knocked it down, I responded in the best way every day staying true to my goal of preventing the later development of rheumatoid arthritis yet all the while having life happen to me and people in my life. All things which require a response yet had to be properly judged for the amount of attention given in order to remain productive. To keep the Shawnversation Train moving, I had to rise to the occasion. Life was calling me out.

My reflecting upon what I was doing and what I was going through is what inspired LIFE QUIZ. Life has requirements, Life is alive and she doesn't ask you what you want to do. She calls you out after showing you where you are and puts you on your stage like she put me on mine then I heard her ask me: " Shawn, what are you going to do?"

LAVETTE PUBLISHING LLC.

LIFE QUIZ

Life asks you: What are you going to do?
Life pushes and pulls and requires,
She loses, reproduces, she inspires,
She lends, she gives,
She takes the lives of other organisms so you can live,
Then asks you: What are you going to do...Again.
Life demands water for vegetation,
Giving it to plants who also require sun and carbon dioxide;
Carbon dioxide that you exhale from your use of oxygen you have inhaled;
A demanding cooperation, from both sides.

Life, she's for real, she has requirements,
Elements... things that must come to;
To continue...
To live on,
Things You and I must do.

If you don't she won't;
Meaning life will not get better,
Neglect her and you suffer,
Or you lose her altogether.
Life doesn't do best when we do less,
She harmonizes with your efforts so best is manifest.

Life is not idle, she instructs, she shows and speaks too,
Respond to her how you are required ,
She will never ask you what you "want" to do.
When she calls you out to rise to the occasion,
The beneficiary is you.
She shows you through trial and you grow so you can do your best like we
        need you to.
Working for her common continuance, life is love, you clearly see:
She's a blessing with requirements which never allow you to simply and
        effortlessly Be.

LAVETTE PUBLISHING LLC.

ESCAPING OUR OLD WAYS

Understanding impacts behavior.

Once we know and understand what something is, can do, doesn't do, etcetera it effects how we handle and/or look at the item or action in question.

I wish to shed some light on growth and escaping old habits.

A profound point in the growth process is the moment when we realize we need to; when we see its time for us to mentally grow from something . When its time for us to escape from our "Old way", ushering ourselves into a new era.

Some of us become prisoners, trapped in our old ways, simply because we don't see the nature of the guardians of our old ways who hold us in captivity with these things we are attempting to leave.

It's simple: When you're in prison as long as you are walking around the prison, mingling with your fellow prisoners and remaining in the building assigned to you no guard bothers you. Every few hours they get a head count to make sure they still have you...

Soon as you try to escape though; once you merely run towards or touch the fence surrounding the prison: they're sending everything they have for you; every guard, every Warden, every dog... to bring you back. To hold you. If they hear or suspect that you are plotting an escape they come for you and lock you down in the hole. *You are in custody and will not be lost.*

Likening this to our old ways, You know when it is time to change. You can feel the need for change in your spirit. Once you decide to change, your insecurities are going to try to hold you back; those people and things who reside near, around or are in concert with you and the ways you are currently escaping are going to be attempting to bring you back. Everything will have a voice now. Everything that never bothered you will attempt to keep you captive in the state you are attempting to escape. This is the nature of these guards and their guardianship.

You have to be determined to leave and move on. You know they want you but remind your *Self* what *You* want for you. Take it there – Get out of there and grow to where destiny compels you! Free Yourself!

You were created for Excellence!

REAL WORLD WELCOMING

Welcome to the Real World,

Where few things happen the way you plan them. Where you can practice and practice and practice then go on the field to run the play in a game and, even if it works, it doesn't happen exactly the way you practiced.

Welcome to the Real World where laws govern our existence; where man thinks he creates when truly he's a gardener, manager or architect at his best. People are the original person's offspring and seeds fall from plants already here, but no seed do we originate here in the real, Realistic world.

Welcome to the Real World where man loves power. Where we need order for our cooperation to work. Here where mischievous spirits sow discord and division, disrespect and dissention, where they teach your children not to listen, where they are ridiculed for grasping and taking heed to lessons you have given them about the Real World.

Here where in some rooms true intelligence is shunned, where ignorance is funny, where misunderstandings don't find a compromising point but become violent, where greed lives. Where the greed is for paper made from trees which is valuable because we believe and the fruits and vegetables
we trade for are overlooked, In this world where fronting is not always considered backwards.

The Real World welcomes you here where you have to pay attention. Where you're going to learn something whether you try to or not. The Real World where you are more than an accident, habit or a snack. Where it's up to you to make due with the intangibles you were given, where you have to make the best of what you've got, Here, with us: In The Real World.

YARD ENVY

The grass may appear to be greener
On the other side,
As you look the appearance intensifies,
So you go there,
And now that you are here
You find,
The same thing which was there
The entire time.
A Blade.
Or... Blades.
Different but one in the same,
The variation being found in how they are raised;
How they are maintained:
The yards...
So more than likely if you take care of what's here,
You'll stay there:
Finding what's best for you in your own yard.

LAVETTE PUBLISHING LLC.

MOCKERY

Half-heartedly;
As in not whole-heartedly;
Giving effort partially:
Mockery.
Limiting the possibility;
Preventing what could be,
By not doing anything,
When one knows how it should be:
Happening.
Being asked to go the distance,
Then one agrees to go the distance,
Yet behind your back they go half the distance.
Speaking it yet never intending to go the distance.
Not whole-heartedly.
As in giving effort partially;
Half-heartedly:
Mockery.

LAVETTE PUBLISHING LLC.

IRONED OUT

Let the pressure bless you;
Allow those miscellaneous experiences you go through to be worn by you;
They become pins, in the end, on the uniform upon you;
It isn't over until it's over, overcoming is incumbent of you.
The pressure will bring the best from you,
The heat will iron you out;
So don't grow weary in the clutch- stand up:
Victories, accolades and accomplishments are what you're about.
Decorate your resume' with resilience,
Being inclined, even in a loss, for winning;
Cause Life's lessons will teach you- And nothing can ultimately defeat you:
You only become a failure when you allow yourself to.
So don't get lost in the field,
Make it back in,
And from the obstacle you have overcome:
Decorate your ironed uniform with a pin.

LAVETTE PUBLISHING LLC.

KNOWN MISUNDERSTANDING

Do you think I feel good to know,
That You (Fresh from the Academy) are so gung-hoe,
With your training for perps, Jane and John Doe's,
And shot after shot taken at the range putting holes in shadows:
Should I feel good, since I know?
I mean should I be commuting with ease,
Since Your shooting those silhouettes is practice for me,
With you on edge to shoot and not be shot,
And my 9 to 5 working ass can be shot at a routine traffic stop?
Am I okay? Or should I be?
What should I say?
Am I hallucinating or paranoid,
When what you get away with must be okay;
I witness your being brought to justice for killing me,
You leave the courtroom unsentenced,
Wait...a sentence was written...
But it was written in favor of You...and not dead ass me!
You killed me in the streets...
Is justice out here too?
Should court be held in the streets?
I don't think we see it in the courtroom.
Should I feel good that I know You know,
And after your trial you wipe your brow,
"Whew, you saved my ass on this one" – You say,
While an entire Nation cannot understand how.

GRAMMAR

Writing words gives words power;
Words capture memories,
Words describe identities,
Words give us history.
Words teach, instruct and declare.
Words allow us to communicate what is supposed to be: There.
Word power, there are messages in multiple word's definitions;
Words Judge you and can write you into confinement: at sentencing.
Sentencing.
No matter the vernacular the outcome is direction;
From what they say you've done to where you're heading;
From what they suspected to where you will be placed;
Their grammatical structure will write your life away.
Correction: You will be here but you will be gone;
Alive yet not present, being counted...
Far away from home.
Sentencing isn't what you deserve:
Be counted here amongst the free!
Read the words which will teach you, capture words which will empower
    you,
Write your life as a factor in our history.

LAVETTE PUBLISHING LLC.

YELLOW IS GREEN

Yellow is the, yellow is the:
Yellow is the new Green;
Cause your Go and my Go are similar,
But definitely not the same thing;
Since you are not certain,
You're satisfied with only going halfway;
Halfway like: half doing it, halfway proceeding,
Meaning halfway getting paid.
Your Go isn't green- it's yellow,
Not verde - it's armarillo;
You're not using the blessings you were blessed with,
Your green may go forward but its slow.
We need you to transmute your capability into full fledged ability;
Transmutation is a shifting of power, you're capable: Use your energy!
Find your way through understanding then begin applying.
You already know that if you have wings then you are supposed to be
        flying.
So get out the nest Give us your best,
Get your Go Going and puff out your chest,
Stand up on life cause it aint over yet,
Make us Go Harder with the Example You Set.

LAVETTE PUBLISHING LLC.

MY KINDA GUY

It's imperative that I am my kinda guy;
Sincerely narrated: I must value my try;
Even if you compare me, I am me authentically:
All me, all day, I am so I.
My life is a work, my words are my legacy,
My fingertips leave my fingerprints,
What I touch I enhance,
Intentionally:
Consciously, simply because I strive the incline;
In the midst of it going down,
I'm still going up,
Greatness begins in the mind.
Work with me cause I don't do this perfectly,
I practice, grow and learn just like you;
My effort is alive, my strenuous needs reaffirmation,
And when I sit down in there it's liable to smell too.
Still I live as my kinda man,
I give you my best, I am who I am,
I take pride in my work – it's me, all I:
In the skin that I'm in: My Kinda Guy.

WORD PROBLEM

Come face to face with the problem;
Get the problem in front of you;
From there, once you identify the problem:
You can see what it is you can and must do.
The answer is wrong,
When the equation is wrong,
Cause if you've written it wrong,
Then you're solving it wrong;
Since even if you solved,
The problem which isn't,
The numbers don't matter,
When your answer doesn't fix it.
Your answer can't fix it,
And its not that you can't add
Or subtract, multiply or divide numbers
Its simply how you've written the equation you have.
Evaluate the facts,
It may require you to think
Then once you have it down correctly,
It'll be as simple as One, Two, Three.

DREAMS OF IMPERFECTION

Be mine like a gift,
Lend me all of you,
All You is who I need you to be,
As I return my Me back to you.
Provide me with exclusive love,
A love only you possess,
Love me with all of what your spirit allows,
Love me proud, where I puff up my chest;
And stand... I'm the man,
In my own little world,
Loved by a wonderful woman,
Not a growing undeveloped girl.
I need the balancing you bring,
The completion you represent;
Be the absent rib I was born without,
Bless me with a presence which keeps me content.
We were meant to be who we are here to be,
With our Us drawing us nearer to our purpose.
Let us write it wonderfully and script it imperfect.
Imperfect because we may miss our lines,
We may even fall climbing the steps;
Yet what's profound is we live and love our lives,
This characteristic makes it best.

LAVETTE PUBLISHING LLC.

EXPOUND

Expound upon life;
Present yourself and go hard;
Speak You through what you do:
Make a statement with who you are.
Expound as in get in it;
In it as in to draw greatness out;
Greatness in how you are living:
Be a force we can't live without.
Expound like give meaning;
Meaning in your demonstration;
Demonstrating excellence:
The excellence for which you were created.
Cause when you take in all the facts,
Then you add in all your gifts,
Then you grow with your abilities giving your best,
The result will be you've expounded.

LAVETTE PUBLISHING LLC.

ALPHA SEED

The Garden must Be.
The Garden is life;
The essence of our existence,
The universal horticulture of you and I.
What do I mean? What did I say:
Without the seed there would be no today,
Since there would be no plants you would not exist;
And your egg wouldn't have developed unless the seed germinated it.
But you did and you grew,
You became and you Are,
You strive for higher levels,
You are a star;
You become if you're not,
Since you know what you've got,
And you learn what you don't,
Cultivating the ingredients within your pot.
Your person is an ever growing seed,
Malleable and productive and able to be
All of which you condition it to be,
Train your You: mentally and physically;
Cause "they" is they and that is not you,
And you don't have be their profile if you don't want to,
And you don't have to fit their stereotype,
You are You, a Garden, from a seed, permeating life.

LAVETTE PUBLISHING LLC.

XYZ

We can give you the letters,
But you have to make them your's,
From there you must compose the letters,
Then turn them into words.
Words that are already here...
Is what you get next,
You get those words for free,
Yet you must claim what you possess.
You possess them once you take them in,
They become yours once you comprehend,
You comprehend then you share,
The vocabulary you have,
In your safe up there.
This ability you have for communicating,
Is the foundation of the training you're obtaining,
Yet to reach your great expectations you must desire,
To feed your safe with understanding to take you higher.
Higher as in being able to reach in your mind,
Like the magician places his arm in the hat to find,
That the usefulness of all that's been placed in there,
Can be drawn out at will and take you there.
There as in demonstrating from the training with ABC,
In the beginning, that led you to the XYZ.
Taking you from letters, to words, to books, all three,
To learning, to understanding, then ability.

LAVETTE PUBLISHING LLC.

STAGE LIGHTS…..

On the night that I sit here and write this commentary about Stage Lights… don't you know that your man Shawn had been faced with a situation where I had to stunt. I had to upgrade the whip(car). When my car is great given what I've been through in life. I read this piece(written earlier this year) And it reminded me that I need to be grateful and maintain, don't lose focus. The mission isn't even about the car, the car is a tool to transport you through the land daily taking steps towards the mission, not to be another member crossing the stage in the parade.

This Shawnversation collection is a reminder for those who need a reminder. I needed to read this after what I did on 5-29-2018.

I've been on the stage, caught up in it. I have to be clean but being clean isn't what life is all about. I get caught up in showing up with the right glow too so don't take this like I can judge you. Take it from a person who has been caught up in being fly that life isn't only about that. Maybe I'm just reminding myself.

Sometimes I say that I wore the same white and blue outfit for 14 years, I have to get some new clothes every now and then right? New shoes, hats, accessories… or is it for the Stage Lights

LAVETTE PUBLISHING LLC.

STAGE LIGHTS

Stage lights, stage fright and being impressive,
Big time, big grind to reach the stage.
Alright now that I have possessions,
In line for my shine in the parade.
Putting myself in debt to impress,
Yet not looking at it flaw so long as I survive.
Late on the lights, but I'm alright,
Since the way I'm looking, I can't help but shine.
Don't know if I'm superficial but I'll say I ain't,
Cause I'm going to be fly like this even if I can't.
What I'm saying is I'm clean even if I have to get dirty,
So when they look at me they're going to know I'm worthy.
Worthy appearance but I don't know what I value,
Since I'm wrapped up in the pursuit of my stuff or what have you;
I mean I can't understand why I go so hard,
When the love of money is frowned upon by God.
Truthfully I've pondered if it's really true that I
Spend money I don't have on things I don't need to impress people that I
       really do not like.
But for now I'm on stage and I see it alright,
In the parade to be captured by the stage lights.

LAVETTE PUBLISHING LLC.

ALL THAT

You look and you know,
You can feel it in your chest;
Cause the look, how she glows,
You can sense she's the best.
"I just know- I just know",
Is the best you can say;
There's a certainty within you,
And she's made your day.
You can tell by the way that she walks that she's got it,
And after having her present you don't want to be without it;
It's that *It,* that *HER,* the H-E-R,
A splendid occurrence ...unmatched: by far.
She has presence, composure and voltage in her eyes,
Its electric and her current sends a charge down my spine;
I'm alive, more so now since she's given me power,
Inspiration and courage, I will never Ever cower.
Cause she's just the right amount of what I don't have,
With her I have purpose, but I smile and I laugh;
I'm inspired, I go harder and higher I go,
I achieve things that make me realer than your superhero.
What I mean is I learn and I work and provide,
Upon her, my earth, I make sure my sun shines,
Individually, I make sure I contribute my seed,
She receives it and transforms it into a continuation of me.
So for what she can do I do what I can do,
And for what she *can't* do I do what I can do.
She fits the description of who I'm telling you about,
She's the epitome of all that I can't live without.
She's sensual and sexy with authentic symmetry,
She's a woman and a lady with respectable integrity;
She has the presence you didn't know you'd desire as a child,
With fire in her eyes and a heartwarming smile.
She's got sense and understanding – noteworthy charisma,

LAVETTE PUBLISHING LLC.

And she speaks like she's right here on the earth with ya.
She's the show you hurry home to sit down and watch;
While scrolling your timeline, she's the reason you stop:
To glance awhile longer to witness her magnificence,
To comprehend what she meant by the things she just posted.
She's captivating and cool and for all that I missed:
She is all of that, plus all of this.

LAVETTE PUBLISHING LLC.

PROMISES

You said you could and you would;
You had me convinced that you should;
Should like you were able yet you are incapable,
You didn't...but... you promised.
I don't remember how far you made it,
I just know you didn't reach the destination.
You didn't arrive at our chosen location,
Where you said we would go, we didn't take it;
You said you would never disappoint,
And even when you did I was a good sport about it;
If that's what you call it when you put your effort and passion on the line,
Then you lose and have to prepare for a new opponent next time.
We were a team, so it seemed,
Destined to take our unity to the championship;
Yet you couldn't continue – I mean you wouldn't,
I guess you had already drawn what you needed from the relationship.
Or was it that your intentions could never match your practice?
Could it be that you wouldn't give it even though you had it;
Holding on to the past, protecting yourself from me,
When you and I is what I believed we had?
I don't know your side of the story,
I do know that you never made it;
Yet I am reluctant to find you to discover another story,
The story of how you promised but couldn't take it.
Couldn't take it where you said, couldn't live your words
Even though you still live.
I take it you couldn't even if you promised and didn't,
I will – it is what it is.

LAVETTE PUBLISHING LLC.

TIME DIFFERENCE...

This one is meant to shed a deeper light on individuality. There is only one you. Only one me. We make this garden called earth work through cooperation in similar manners yet our lanes are not the same and can never truly be the "same".

We each have our responsibilities and as managers we have to manage what requires our management. We definitely have to manage who we are. We have time to do. Time here. Time to live on the planet before our expiration date arrives. We have to live, live as in live up. Time is fleeting by nature and you can't get her back. We are all serving time.

I know people who have had the circumstances in which they serve their time here be written into confined conditions. All from what is called a crime against the people. All of them dream for the freedom you have. Some are preparing themselves for a better life daily by doing what they can to be better daily even if on paper it says they will never see being free again. They understand they have time to do here and chose to do it, awake, well and improving, making the best of the circumstances surrounding them. Choosing to be better.

I share this cause the places are different yet the concept is similar: what do you need to do your time here? How are you going to get it in a way where it doesn't make your time hard? Is it making you better? What are you doing to grow to be better? What can you do? Do it. There is always an option.

You were created for excellence and you innately strive to be the best at whatever you do. Choose to become closer to your individual excellence during some point in every day that the day has you.

LAVETTE PUBLISHING LLC.

TIME DIFFERENCE

There is a difference in time, and you are not doing mine;
You can't do mine- Why? Cause it's mine.
You have yours and I have my time, there's a difference.
Do your time: I hope that you get it.
I don't have a twin;
But even if I did,
He is not me and I am not him,
What I have is mine and what he has belongs to him.
The difference is that he is alive;
Alive for a written amount of time,
Blessed with an allotted time to live;
Mortality is real and his is all his.
Yours is all yours, the concept is the same;
In a world full of highways, I have my own lane;
A lane in life that it is imperative that I maintain;
So even if our time started around the same time our time is not the
        same.
You are unique.
I don't use the bathroom from what you eat;
Even if I helped you get the food on your plate,
Your food is yours even if we share a fork and eat from the same tray.
You are an identity, a person, individually,
All you all day you are not none of me.
Your wealth and your health are under your ownership,
My physical fitness doesn't improve from the weights you lift.
It is all the way important that I awaken every day,
Grateful for the beginning of yet another day,
On Go as I proceed and intend to be great,
Be productive in my gardening, own and fix my mistakes.
Cause since I see that my body is not perfect,
I exercise and work it to improve my imperfect;
And since I understand what it means to sow and reap,
I go out and work in the garden so me and mine can eat.

LAVETTE PUBLISHING LLC.

Sometimes the difference in time is only a shift in perspective,
An enhancement, broadening a mind, lending direction.
A boss that doesn't understand how to lead is only in the way,
And one can't do the job if they can't use the tools that it takes.
Uplift you and gift yourself with ability,
You were blessed with position, potential and capability.
It's going to take for you to know what you can do,
With an open-mind to know what you need to learn to do;
To exist and maintain with what is best for you,
With everything working you will serve yours yet time will serve you.
Fulfillment arrives when you understand the laws,
Laws of your being and how everything works for just cause;
Functioning for your benefit what you do is beneficial as well,
You are not lost and you are not under a spell.
You understand the gift found in the present;
You are also aware that your being alive is a blessing;
Making a difference here by doing your time is what you do,
Living sincerely, not allowing your time to do you.

LAVETTE PUBLISHING LLC.

SEND

Once you press SEND,
Its gone, the end;
The words are going to land,
No matter what you intend;
No taking it back,
It is what it is;
What you said is on the way:
Once you press SEND.
If we aren't considerate of what we intend to say,
Our words may cause our intentions to be betrayed,
A situation where we didn't mean to say what we said,
With what we just wrote correctly being incorrectly read.
Or could it be words sprouting from an incomplete understanding,
Where the words came exactly how you planned it,
Where their words or actions came and you body-slammed it,
Now you are willing to wrestle what's next now that they have it?
What I find myself doing is pumping my brakes,
Giving myself time with what I intend to say,
Allowing myself a moment to comprehend what they said,
Being real enough to ask them to clarify what I just read.
I simply wish for my conversation to be understood;
With when I share my words with you, you get what you should;
Rooted in my wanting my intentions, actions and words to compliment,
So when I send my words you get what you are supposed to get.
I mean once you press SEND, it is what it is;
Your words are going to land no matter what you intend.
What you said is on the way, its gone, the end;
No taking it back once you press SEND.

MOVING CREW

Big bags, big boxes, big cars, big house,
Big love seat, big shoes, big socks, big couch,
Big plans, wrong man, wrong woman, get out,
Move up, move on, Go, just move out.
What you take with you from what he did with you,
May be in the way as you go where life leads you,
Since your new relationship is new like brand new,
You may be better off abandoning some of the baggage he leaves you.
And I know its unbelievable the way that she did you,
Apparently it seems like she practically used you.
Through turbulence and turmoil you strived to provide,
Yet find she creeping with a man who's unemployed the whole time.
I mean he can't save her or give her a dime;
Or put gas in the car you graciously provide;
Provided cause you want it and you want back your promise ring,
The watch, matching bracelet and a list of other things.
You say she can't but its obvious that she did,
Now you are moving on like the woman in the beginning did,
Who got sick of his promises which were left unfulfilled,
She felt caged and trapped in a relationship headed towards a dead end.
Yet now that its over she's truly trying to move,
She saw through the mess in his mess now that its over- she's through.
Big bags, big boxes, clothes must be packed;
On a truck put the chest of drawers- you need all that.
We know like you know you can't get back the time you spent,
But don't let past times steal new time, news flash: New Relationship.
You can pack up your things and leave the baggage behind,
Don't let it ride with you, it can't fit in your ride.

GOOD

How does it feel?
Good.
Like okay;
Like right.
Right not right like go that way;
But right like going the right way.
Good?
Yes;
It's a feeling inside;
Not inside, inside like not outside;
But inside like within your body, in your mind.
Good;
Like more profound than just touch feel it,
But good in a greater sense you can feel in your spirit;
Its heightened like righteous as in no doubt about it;
Feels righteous going down as in you are certain about it.
Certain about how good it is,
No matter what it is,
You can simply feel:
Its good.

STAT ENHANCEMENT

They handed you a stat like that would be it;
Gave you a statistic like you had to define it;
Gave you some numbers like these are your cards,
You challenged the odds since numbers don't define who you are.
You are not defined by gender or color,
You are one of a kind, not one of another,
Who owns your own brain, own eyes and heart,
Who is more than collected data saying who you are.
They named you a statistic and you kindly accepted,
You took that into your room and blessed it;
Then came out your room and went straight to the kitchen,
And decided you were going to eat their statistic.
Determined, were you, to eat their stat;
You'd burn more calories if they said you were fat,
You'd grind until you became physically fit,
Meaning their stat came out and you transformed it.
You let the world hand you what they thought was a lemon,
What they figured you'd be stuck with once you get it,
But you were fortunate enough to see the blessing within it,
Broke the lemon down and made lemonade with it.
You took their stat and while in the kitchen,
You learned and reasoned and seasoned it didn't
Get caught up in the fact you didn't get "their" classes,
Your classification became opportunity: stat enhancement.

HEAD SCREEN...

This one is just me having fun after I had an encounter with an individual and I encouraged them to have a nice day when have a nice day isn't what I wanted to say.

This is just a show that everything doesn't require your attention. Every action has a reaction and in the case of the message found in my encouraging the person to have a nice day all they could do is be stunned and keep it moving.

LAVETTE PUBLISHING LLC.

HEAD SCREEN

If my mind had a screen,
And everything I thought could be seen,
I mean visible like a billboard like on a big screen,
I'd probably die, cause I would just think and you'd see.
You'd see what I thought yet didn't say,
My screen would articulate thoughts I couldn't communicate;
Clearly. Scary cause I was trying to keep a secret,
Attempting to conceal my hand but you peeped it;
You seen it, even if I lied or denied or tried,
You could put two and two together and see why.
It would be terrible when I respond to my kids,
She'd ask: "Isn't this pretty daddy?" and the screen reads YOU NEED TO
    TRY THAT AGAIN;
When I meant to say: "Baby I love it!"
Cause I can't say my daughter's drawing is ugly.
Not in public; no public, we must be politically correct;
I don't need my head's screen helping me get it off my chest,
Since there is no telling what the the screen would say,
When you have tested my nerves but I stated "Have a nice day!"
This screen ain't right cause the truth can be so wrong,
I know I have rights, but I'm trying to get along,
And travel peacefully as I make my commute,
And not have my Head's Screen tell you exactly what I might do.

LAVETTE PUBLISHING LLC.

OPAQUE

I'm not here;
Not here for you to see;
Not saying that you can't see,
But saying that you can't see me.
Here I stand,
Standing upon both ...both of my feet;
Standing here visible... yet in all truth I'm invisible:
Invisible as invisibility can possibly be.
Cause its me.
Compare me to a tree;
Saying that it's the tree you see,
But you cannot fully envision all of what makes me the tree be;
Be as in what comprises me,
What makes me logistically,
As in the functioning
The struggle
The development
The hustle,
The devotion
The consciousness
And The Will which gives me ability:
You can't see me.
Cause these things make me
And you may hate me
But you will never break me
Cause I've been determined since He created me.
Determined to be here,
Born prematurely,
Early, yes Early,
But you don't see me.
So critique me
Be cynical and tell me what can't be,
And tally up your odds,
Statistics that I shall most surely beat and, or defeat.

LAVETTE PUBLISHING LLC.

And when you see what I do
Know what I did;
Know what it is when it's my fruit you see;
Use my fruit to judge me;
What I produce to judge me.
But you can't budge me
Nudge me or better yet push me:
Cause here I stand,
Attempting to help you understand,
That you can't see me.

LAVETTE PUBLISHING LLC.

LETTER

Break up with broken mentalities;
Divorce dilapidated realities;
Marry the desire to be your best,
Make success your reality.
Be that You that only you can be;
Embrace greatness when it summons you,
You will have to rise to the occasion to meet your greater self,
Choose to win, the ultimate victories will not just come to you.
Be victorious you great person you,
Make greatness synonymous with your existence;
Condition your spectacular like an exercise,
Work out towards a great human being's existence.
Make it apparent in your demonstration;
Seek, understand, apply and teach.
Be all you personally, have that aura,
Compel your excellence to be achieved.
The tortoise taught us we can still win,
If we remain steadfast.
Strive towards all which is best for you,
Your best can never be considered last.
Leave a losing predisposition,
Enjoin habits which make you better,
Mold yourself into the mind frame of winning,
Live up to your greatness through each and every letter.

LAVETTE PUBLISHING LLC.

MORE

I am not a short story,
I am not a novel: I am a series.
I require more than a page in a book,
I take up a section of books: in the library;
A page turning, lesson learning suspense filled thriller,
Encyclopedias transcribed describing the life of a determined go-getter.

If you wanted to produce me and make me a song,
Then it wouldn't work out cause I would play too long.
You can't put one me on one single track;
Just to cover the highlights I need a soundtrack.
I am, I am a collection of jams;
In pursuit of eternity on Sixteens I land,
And come from my lips with profound hits;
On the One's and Two's, Shawnversation: The It.

I leave you with my Me in a way,
That once the two and two come together you know its okay,
And I never did nothing but live and learn,
To grow up and man up until the dirt is where I return.

LAVETTE PUBLISHING LLC.

YOU ALREADY KNOW

Deception and discord is the way of the Devil,
We need you to man up and bring us together.
Since you already know the intent is to keep us separated,
Then be united if you are brave enough to take it.
Already, if you know you have been profiled,
That you are a deadbeat and you will not raise your child,
You're a hoodlum? Drug dealer, nothing more than a criminal?
Why don't you take the brush in your hands and paint a better picture?
Since you know that how they act about you isn't fact,
Why not have integrity and show you not that?
Since all amounts of affliction stand to enhance you,
Shouldn't you embrace your trials and demand a better you?
Since you know you are going to always need some money,
And food aint free and the bills are going to keep coming,
Until life leads you to a retirement chair,
Shouldn't you learn you some abilities to take you there?
I mean you already know that your world is a farm,
And everything grows and requires your arm,
And your hand and you man to help manage it,
Shouldn't you find you a spot so you can be amongst the management?
You are not a fake You, you really are alive,
Not a manufactured version, you are one of a kind,
There will never be another you, you tell us that a lot,
So have us know you've given us all that you've got.

LAVETTE PUBLISHING LLC.

INVISIBLE

Invisible...
Thats what you wish I would be;
Simply so you will not see,
Or witness the gifts which I was blessed with which lend me excellent
      intangibility;
I mean intangibles, my qualities
My who I cannot help but be;
So what you wish is in conflict with what must inevitably be.
If I were invisible like air, you wouldn't see me there,
Even though my presence is a necessity.
I am here, I am there, I am all around,
That is how I am supposed to be.
I was created and I am a splendid invention,
I am grateful for life and capability.
I know that I can, I am man, I can grow
To transform capable to able as in ability.
I cannot be invisible, I am indivisible,
I am a presence, I am all Me.
More than a number, I am a factor,
I think and comprehend and extend my understanding to those who come
      near me.
There is no such thing as an invisible manager,
Our Creator, The Owner, put me here to lead;
To worship Him, reproduce, manage our sustenance,
He put man here to be King.
So King: don't leave, or disappear,
Develop your excellence;
The manifestation of why you're here will be clear,
Don't be invisible as they wish.

LAVETTE PUBLISHING LLC.

PERSPECTIVE - PERCEPTION

Perspective
Depends on where you are;
Your position, as in where you stand,
Where you see it from,
Your view of what you're attempting to completely understand.
Under Stand, as in foundation;
The base of how you comprehend,
All of which effects your vision,
The perspective from which floor of the building you are in.
Perspective like your level in the stands,
Allowing you to read the message spelled by the band,
You may not be able to read the word,
If on the field level is where you stand.
If you are not up there you are just not there,
Not on the level where you can see.
It requires for you to elevate- to become higher,
To be in position to visualize what you've just seen.
Perception, Perception, Perception
The manner in which I see;
The how I see what I just saw,
How that effects what it means... to me.
One word can have various meanings,
 Their definition interpreted from the tone,
So an event can be miscomprehended,
If our perception of the event is wrong.
Perception of an item can affect how we behave;
Let's say the man thinks the money makes him, when he must make the
        money
When money makes him it enslaves,
It will awaken his darkside just so it can be obtained.
Perspective is all about where you are,
Whether it be physically, mentally or spiritually;
Perception is similar yet not the same

LAVETTE PUBLISHING LLC.

Its more about the interpretation of what you're witnessing.
Yet when we take a step back for comprehension purposes,
We find the true meanings which we need,
Even though we always need the truth to assist our reactions,
I'm enhancing how we see by 2 words which start with P.

LAVETTE PUBLISHING LLC.

FATHER'S DAY

We can't choose our parents,
Yet, I am grateful God chose you for me;
Since you always lend understanding,
Regardless of what the trial may be.
There are countless Dads with great characteristics,
There are those who are just who they are,
But this is a tribute... for You:
For every great thing that You Are!
I cannot compare you to their's,
I am thankful that you're mine,
With the consistent way you care,
And the best from within me which you inspire;
For the Patriarch that you are,
On your Day, I embrace you gladly;
I salute You: General, King, My Father...
You: Daddy.

LAVETTE PUBLISHING LLC.

A LETTER

To Whom It May Concern:

This letter is a calling to your inner Greatness from your present inspiration Mr. Shawnversation.

I am writing this from the perspective of a concerned teammate who wants to win with his team. We all are here playing together on the planet earth until our expiration date arrives; when our end comes. Right now I want to talk about the beginning so our inception can be the move of a person conscious and focused on winning.

Mankind was given an entire planet which functions for his benefit. Sometimes we as a people see a garden and we scoff at it. The thought of garden work makes a lot of us become standoffish about if we are truly willing to do the work when gardening is vital to our survival.

The fact of the matter is that the world is a garden. The technology surrounding you came from the ground. Mankind has grown to understand the properties of the various organisms and elements on the planet and transformed their inherent laws into valuable items which make our lives enjoyable, easier and enriching. The facts show it all comes from the ground. It all comes from the Garden. Man was created to tend to the Garden.

Each and every one of us were blessed with the capacities necessary for us to be successful contributors to the work required for life to continue. The brain we have affords us the chance we need to learn. We learn how to make our little contribution mean something. Our ability to love allows us to care and take pride in what we were put here to do, making it enriching to have our loves ones satisfied by our efforts in assisting their survival. If you don't work, you don't eat.

The basic laws of existence have everything functioning with or without you, but if we don't work with those laws, as in manage them for our benefit, we can never bring what we need home.

My intent with this letter is to put the basics on the table cause even though we say we know we don't all act like we know. I just want to remind you so you can win in this game of life with me and I can win with you.

The world is a garden which you possess.

LAVETTE PUBLISHING LLC.

I FEEL ME is the last one I wrote for this collection. May this piece remind you of the struggle we all go through to achieve. I know I wrote XYZs earlier during the completion of this project but here I remind you that once you get the XYZs which is figurative for understanding they require you to maintain now that you know. There is a responsibility found in our finding our way.

Life is forever replenishing itself. Its always growing and making a way for you. It's also always dying too; For your continuation, so live.

I identify with all of you who have had to try twice as hard just to maintain and this is for you. For you who think it can't be done I am here to tell you it can always be done you just have to want to its on you. Don't give up. Don't lose hope. Do what you can. The seeds you plant will grow while no one else can see (like I said in the first piece in this collection) and once your seed blossoms it will be awe inspiring. Give your garden the proper attention.

Don't be misled by the confusion out here. Get to know that person in the mirror and develop. Feel that person. You feel You, even if they don't, they don't have to.

LAVETTE PUBLISHING LLC.

I FEEL ME

You look me in my eyes,
But you not feeling me in your chest,
Cause you don't know when I tried,
Yet I lost when the competition wasn't near to being the best.
You don't know what its like,
You never lost your life and didn't die;
You weren't criminalized,
You never fought to be a citizen, they didn't loophole your rights.
You don't feel me in your heart when you look me in my eyes;
You didn't rehabilitate yourself from being institutionalized;
What you know about working for free and not being a volunteer?
Convincing yourself you're developing a work ethic cause you're gonna be
          free when you make it up outta here.
You don't feel me, I can tell by your attitude,
You never struggled to learn the ABC's
Only to grow to need the XYZ's
Then you get them to see they require you to be on your P's and Q's.
When you look me in my eyes,
You must be hoping I won't try,
It isn't going to be made easy for me to have mine,
You know I go twice as hard to be able to buy.
I'm living my life, standing upright,
Nutritious amongst social poisons,
There's a certainty there when you know that you're right,
You wake up motivated in the morning.
You can look all you will,
You don't have to feel,
You can't piss down my back and tell me its rain no more;
I have my reality and my life and I choose to live:
And I feel me, even if you don't.

LAVETTE PUBLISHING LLC.

22559102R00033